Quiet Spaces

The brf prayer and spirituality journal

Tomorrow

Edited by Heather Fenton

Text copyright © BRF 2011
Authors retain copyright in their own work

Published by
The Bible Reading Fellowship
15 The Chambers
Abingdon, OX14 3FE
United Kingdom
Tel: +44 (0)1865 319700
Email: enquiries@brf.org.uk
Website: www.brf.org.uk
BRF is a Registered Charity

ISBN 978 1 84101 661 0
First published 2011
10 9 8 7 6 5 4 3 2 1 0

Acknowledgments
Scripture quotations taken from The Holy Bible, New International Version, copyright © 1973, 1978, 1984 by International Bible Society, are used by permission of Hodder & Stoughton, a member of the Hachette Livre UK Group. All rights reserved. 'NIV' is a registered trademark of International Bible Society. UK trademark number 1448790.

Scripture quotations taken from The New Revised Standard Version of the Bible, Anglicised Edition, copyright © 1989, 1995 by the Division of Christian Education of the National Council of the Churches of Christ in the USA, and are used by permission. All rights reserved.

Extracts from the Authorised Version of the Bible (The King James Bible), the rights in which are vested in the Crown, are reproduced by permission of the Crown's patentee, Cambridge University Press.

Scripture quotations taken from the Contemporary English Version of the Bible, published by HarperCollins Publishers, are copyright © 1991, 1992, 1995 American Bible Society.

Scriptures quoted from the Good News Bible published by The Bible Societies/HarperCollins Publishers Ltd, UK © American Bible Society 1966, 1971, 1976, 1992, used with permission.

Scripture quotations from The Message. Copyright © by Eugene H. Peterson 1993, 1994, 1995. Used by permission of NavPress Publishing.

A catalogue record for this book is available from the British Library

Printed in the UK by Harcourt Litho

VOLUME 18
Contents

Tomorrow

The Editor writes...

Heather Fenton is the Editor of *Quiet Spaces*.

It is getting towards evening now. The shadows are lengthening. Questions like 'What shall we have for supper?' become more urgent. Soon we will have to decide and act upon that decision. It may be a good idea to look at the calendar or in the diary soon, too—just to check that I know if there is anything particular I am expected to do tomorrow or still need to prepare for. So tomorrow creeps up on us and, to some extent, we must prepare for it. The time for keeping it firmly in the 'future' is getting short.

Tomorrow may not hold any particular surprises but we will soon be there. So it is with our human lives, which can seem an endless chain of 'tomorrows'. Some are painful, some exciting, but most are somewhere in between.

This issue of *Quiet Spaces* is dedicated to the theme of 'Tomorrow'. We begin with Andrew Jones, who lives on the Welsh coast at Llanbedrog and is therefore on the pilgrimage route to the island of Bardsey. The deep theological idea of 'seeking one's place of resurrection' is at the heart of the practice of pilgrimage and Andrew helps us to see that seeking this place in the contemporary context means three interrelated things: faithful stability, an authentic security and, ultimately, a well-balanced lifestyle. 'For each one of us, the journey will be different, and the route towards tomorrow and our own place of resurrection… will be one that we must each discover for ourselves.'

We stay on that same pilgrimage route, this time moving west to Aberdaron, the departure place for Bardsey, where pilgrims have to 'let go' of the land and cross the notorious 'Bardsey Sound'. It is here that Jim Cotter works, and his writings spring from his own experiences. Jim writes a kind of meditation on letting go as we get older: '… less clutter, more simplicity, more conviviality; less clatter, more silence… '

Marion Gray knows that living in today but being aware of tomorrow is not always easy. What did Jesus mean when he said, 'Do not worry about tomorrow, for tomorrow will bring worries of its own'? She reminds us that Jesus warned us not to worry about the future but he also encouraged his listeners to think ahead and count the cost; to build on the rock, not on the sand; to seek heavenly treasure, forgive past wrongs and mend relationships, as these are all things that make us fit for tomorrow.

Exploring one of the great passages of scripture that draws us 'beyond tomorrow', David Spriggs helps us to look at Revelation 21–22, which contains 'what is perhaps the greatest image of new creation'. As we explore some of the depths behind this passage, we can see how the intentions of God, the glimpsed experiences of God's people and the daring vision of the prophet are gathered together seamlessly within John's portrayal. Through the eyes of this revelation, we can feel the powerful magnetism of God's new future.

Also in this issue we have some resources for small group worship and some material for making a quiet corner that could last from Epiphany to Candlemas. There are other articles, including some poetry and prayers as well as the usual columns, 'Tony's reflections' and 'Margaret's space', plus some space for you to add your own notes, ideas or meditations. So find a quiet place, explore this issue of *Quiet Spaces* and enjoy the opportunities they bring!

ANDREW JONES

Journeying together to seek our place of resurrection

author

Andrew Jones is Archdeacon of Meirionnydd and rector of four churches on the Llyn Peninsula in North Wales. He regularly leads pilgrimages to places in the UK and abroad. He is the author of *Pilgrimage* (BRF, April 2011)—see www.brfonline.org.uk.

My first encounter with the idea of seeking one's own place of resurrection came while reading Meilyr Brydydd's deathbed song with a group of American pilgrims on a cliff overlooking Bardsey Island, just off the Llyn Peninsula in North-West Wales. Meilyr Brydydd was court poet to Gruffudd ap Cynan, a great prince of Gwynedd during the twelfth century. At that time, the court poets were charged primarily with recording in poetry the achievements of their princes—the equivalents of modern-day tabloid reporters, maybe! Towards the end of his song, Meilyr prays that after his imminent death he will find his own resurrection on Bardsey Island.

Those American pilgrims were keen to know more about this idea of 'finding one's own place of resurrection' in particular holy places. As he approaches death, Meilyr Brydydd pleads for God's mercy and seeks peace and reconciliation with God before he dies. In his pleading he shows that he is aware of his own fragility and sense of sinfulness, and he is determined to renew his commitment to God through the power of the incarnation and the intercession of Mary. All of these will eventually, he hopes, assure him of a good death and a glorious resurrection alongside the 20,000 saints claimed by tradition to be buried on Bardsey. What is particularly interesting about this poem is the way in which Meilyr, while seeking his own place of resurrection, also claims that the actual physical island is an inheritor of salvation. As an important place of medieval pilgrimage, Bardsey is itself in expectation of new life—the head of the island pointing eastwards, eagerly awaiting the coming

A journey with and towards God, either alone or in the company of others

of the risen life, the life of Christ's eternal kingdom. Indeed, throughout the Celtic tradition there is a strong sense that the whole of creation, without distinction, can become part of the great family of resurrection.

So this deep theological idea of 'seeking one's place of resurrection' has been at the heart of the practice of pilgrimage since medieval times. For thousands of years, in several traditions and with all kinds of different motives, people have opted to become pilgrims—to embark on a journey with and towards God, either alone or in the company of others. Pilgrims come to sacred places to seek healing, inspiration and redirection. Often it is a quest by simple, practical and concrete-minded people to find 'stepping-stones' between themselves and the geographically distant and spiritually abstract concepts of their particular religious tradition, whether they be Jews, Muslims, Christians, Hindus, Sikhs or Buddhists.

For Christians, the practice of pilgrimage as a way of becoming church

in a different and fresher way is nothing new. It is an experience that has always challenged and continues to challenge the church as an establishment in so many ways. It is no coincidence, I feel, that as the number of people who attend church for worship on Sunday is on a serious decline, the number of people (particularly young people) who flock to traditional places of pilgrimage throughout the world is on an exciting increase. This challenge has often focused on the ambivalent relationship between one's inner spiritual journey of faith towards God and the outward, more physical journey of life on earth. It is in this sense that the outward physical pilgrimage is a sign of an inner journey that seeks resurrection—the journey of the heart, which is held in the Creator's hands. It is rooted in the conviction that life itself is a process of continual change and movement. Christians are never static; they carry within themselves a sense of expectancy, of looking forward in hope. This is what the writer to the Hebrews was referring to when he mentioned 'running with perseverance the race that is set before us' (Hebrews 12:1–2, NRSV). Here is expressed that marvellous pilgrimage of the Christian on a journey into the very heart of God, a pilgrimage that will never be completed here on earth but continues into God's eternal kingdom.

At the heart of the Christian tradition is the conviction that the children of God already live in this world with one foot in the kingdom of God. In the birth, life, ministry, death and resurrection of Jesus, as recorded in the New Testament, the kingdom of God has already been inaugurated. It is not something that lies entirely in the future—a kind of pie in the sky when

> The outward physical pilgrimage is a sign of an inner journey that **seeks resurrection**

you die—and nor is it an experience that can be fully understood and achieved in the here and now. The unfolding of the kingdom of God is both a lifelong experience and a lifelong endeavour that the children of God seek and share with one another and with God himself.

I suppose that an early, possibly Celtic, interpretation of 'seeking one's place of resurrection' would have involved discovering a particularly appealing holy place and imaginatively entering the kingdom of God through that place. Historically, for many people the ultimate point of pilgrimage was to discover the place of one's own resurrection—that is, a physical place

---

The unfolding of the kingdom of God is both a lifelong experience and a lifelong endeavour...

---

in which to die so as to embark on a new adventure. For some early thinkers, the holy place became the divinely appointed place for the pilgrim seeker to settle in, to spend the rest of life there in a state of holy penance and waiting. In an immediate sense, that holy place

was simply a waiting room en route to the eventual place of resurrection, namely heaven. This is the background to appreciating Meilyr Brydydd's love of Bardsey.

The connection, therefore, between particular sacred places, the practice of pilgrimage and the theological idea of seeking one's place of resurrection is a crucially important one. The Christian (particularly Catholic) psyche has, for generations, believed that pilgrimage is not simply a religious holiday with a bit of worship thrown in. Rather, it is a journey where the destination itself is sacred. Standing in these holy destinations of resurrection helps pilgrims to see something of their own resurrection possibility within them. This highly personal perspective of the pilgrim is essential for grasping the depth of participation that true pilgrimage requires.

As a pilgrimage leader, I find that particular places become powerful anchors of faith. This, of course, should not surprise us. In the ancient biblical world, many physical places of pilgrimage were, in fact, closely connected to the stories of salvation: to know the place was to know the story, and to know the story was to know God. The disciples' vision of the resurrected Jesus revealed to them not only the glory of God but also what it means to be most fully human. The greatest surprise of the resurrection was that, in seeing the risen Christ, the disciples saw themselves anew.

Immersed, then, in the complexity and mess of human living, what are we to make of all this today? What exactly does the idea of seeking one's own place of resurrection mean to us in the here and now? My experience with pilgrims nowadays convinces me that to speak in terms of seeking holy places in order to lay down our heads in a kind of sacred penance and patient waiting would be to miss the mark and to risk being branded a religious lunatic. For me, talk about seeking one's own place of resurrection in the contemporary context means three interrelated things.

The first is the most basic and human of them all. Journeying together as pilgrims to a particular holy place affords us a vital opportunity to explore the important things of life and to examine life's priorities in order to seek three things: faithful stability, an authentic security and, ultimately, a well-balanced lifestyle. Far too many people in our so-called comfortable developed Western societies live frantic and frenetic lifestyles, unable to find contentment and true anchorage. Pausing either alone or with others along the pilgrim way to reflect deeply on what it means to be truly human and what it is really like to be immersed in the messy stuff of human living can be frightening. But the legacy of the early saints associated with many of these pilgrim ways continues to be twofold: first, in their day these early saints drew out the sacredness of the land we walk on today, and second, they enable us to use that sacredness to make some crucial connections. Pilgrims are encouraged to connect some of those times and some of those experiences in life when the journey of the heart and the physical pilgrimage of life coincide—the inner and the outer journeys.

To have sought one's own place of resurrection is perhaps the moment

> What exactly does the idea of seeking one's own place of resurrection mean to us in the here and now?

> To have sought one's own place of resurrection is perhaps the moment when this connection is made between a particular experience of life, whether bitter or sweet, and God

when this connection is made between a particular experience of life, whether bitter or sweet, and God. I have found over the years that certain places become places of resurrection because these are the places in which pilgrims find relinquishment. Pausing as a pilgrim in places such as Iona, Glendalough and Holy Island helps the pilgrim to lay a dying mother to rest or to reconsider a broken relationship or to rethink a career or to reclaim a long-lost family or to rediscover stability in life. Here is a way of imagining the possibility of a new life, new beginnings, new perspectives, and to take hold of or seek one's own place of resurrection.

The second related aspect is that places such as St Davids, Durham, Lindisfarne and Canterbury, in particular ways, are very much associated with traditional pilgrimage, but in reality the true pilgrim path is located everywhere and never just in sacred spaces. The question that faces every pilgrim must be: are participants open to being truly *pilgrims*? Are they prepared to live with some of the risks and uncertainties and loose ends that pilgrimage always entails? The pilgrim can never have everything neatly 'sewn up'. There is always the exploration, the search, the movement, the questions, the challenge and the surprise—and these are the very things of both life and resurrection. In this sense, seeking one's own place of resurrection is about allowing space for the unlikely and the extraordinary to happen. One of the big gifts of that first Easter Sunday was the surprise that it gave to the women who came to the grave early to seek the Lord. A carefully ordered and regimented way of life often leaves precious little space for God's surprises to break into our lives. In our seeking of places of resurrection there is an urgent demand to allow time and space through which God's whisper and God's constant surprising can be heard and grasped.

Thirdly, whether the places to which pilgrims journey are places of silence and prayer, of beauty and light, or of imaginative transition from this world to the next, they are all places of precious and irreplaceable gifts. They are all doors through which glimpses of another world can be caught—or better, perhaps, through which another world may reach us. There is, in these places, at least a presence of the past but also a presence of eternity demanding both our reverence and gratitude. Ultimately, it is this third aspect of resurrection places and resurrection surprises that we strive for most.

For each one of us, the journey will be different, and the route towards tomorrow and our own place of resurrection—whether in the sense of seeking balance and authenticity in this life or in the sense of seeking the glory of heaven—will be one that we must each discover for ourselves. Although it is a unique path that faces each of us, it is never a solitary one. The gift of true pilgrimage is that, by arriving at our physical places

Here is a way of **imagining the possibility of a new life**

of destination, we are often surprised to find that the joys and the hopes, the grief and the anguish of our own lives have already been experienced by the people who made those places sacred in the first place. It is often their example and their abiding company that point us forward to tomorrow and to ultimately reaching our own places of resurrection.

JIM COTTER

Letting go

What do you do
when you're asked
for an article
two thousand words long,
and the words peter out?

No more left.
They were let go of
a long time ago.

> The Bible talks of 'the
> **bowels of compassion'**

author

Jim Cotter ministers as
priest-in-charge of Aberdaron
in Wales. He also writes, and
enjoys walking, theatre, and
meeting with friends.

Perhaps they can run down
the middle of each page,
leaving room to breathe
(breathe out, of course you
need space to do that).

Perhaps the result will be
a long column
(like Nelson's?
like a newspaper's?
or like a tower of Babel,
which will topple
if it gets too high?)

Two thousand words
will certainly make it unstable.
So I'll stop this introduction or
justification for
something a bit short
of a thousand.

(I wonder if there'll be
enough room in the magazine,
enough column inches, or
is it millimetres now?
Perhaps you'll be reading this
two columns to a page…)

You loosen your clothing
to sleep,
to make love,
to laugh or cry or roar,
to pray,

to relieve yourself.

The belly needs room to move and
relax.
The Bible talks of 'the bowels of
compassion'.

You can't be compassionate
if you're constipated.
Hebrew is a language

profoundly bodily and spiritual,

both together.
Think about it.
Try not to be

above it all.

You are 'up-tight'.

Only if you let go
can you give in
or out.

Don't hold your breath.
Gently let all the air out.
Trust the air to be there

to fill you again.

Save your life—lose your life.
Lose your life—save your life.

Paradox.
Scratch your head.
What does he mean?

Hold on? Hang on? I've lost it?
But let go? Surely I've still lost it?

Don't hold your breath.
Gently let all the air out.
Trust the air to be there

Thus spoke common sense.

To be rich is to be poor.
To be poor is to be rich.

Hang on a minute.

There he goes again.

That sounds nonsense too.

Of course it is.
Non-sense always is
to common-sense.

Stop playing games with me.

But playing games is what it's about.
Stop being solemn.
Play.

*There is a picture of Winnie-the-Pooh
holding on to a balloon in mid-air*

and a bee buzzing near his nose…

*If you find it hard to trust,
you need to let go of hard-won control,*

and

fall

into

what

looks

like

a

bottomless

pit

of

terror,

but

is

in

truth

an

unfathomable

abyss

of

love where
it
may

fun

learn

be

to

how

to

fly.

… holding on to a balloon in mid-air

Grasp life, cling on to it,
you'll lose it.
Let your life go,
you'll find it.

Less clutter
more simplicity
more conviviality.
Less clatter
more silence
more conversation.
Less chatter
more solitude

more communion.
Fewer things.
Fewer words.

Fewer people.
But they really will matter.

Look after yourself you
will never find yourself.
Forget about yourself you
will find yourself.

Help yourself you
will lose it all.
Give yourself away you
will find it all.

Give yourself away:
all of you,
recklessly,
(can't do that yet)
everything you think you are:
status,

defining you,
possessions,
displaying you,
people,
applauding you.

Get all you want—
lose everything.
Lose all you have find
it all.

Put your own safety first,
you lose everything.
Risk your life for others,
you will really live.

What do you mean?

Think about it.
Work it out.
Test it out.
What do you think matters to you most?
Let it go.

Hah.
Well, try something that matters a
bit.

When you do let go,
'Providence' also moves,
moves towards you
with unexpected gifts.
'Events' seem to happen.

Encounters surprise you
with what you need.
None of it could you have
'dreamt up'.

No need to get 'hung up'
about it all…

Stiff-necked
you try to bear too much.
You are shouldering
too many burdens.
Let Love guide
your embodied being.
Laugh at those who preach grace
and impose duty out of guilt adding
to their own burdens
and trying to add to yours.
Let the Spirit flow through you.
Let the governance be
upon God's shoulders.
Let go…
Let be…
Let God…

Let go in sleep.
Let go into 'le petit mort'.
So prepare to let go
and die into the Mystery.
Be alert to the moment
when you will hear the owl
call your name.

'I find that, for me,
getting nearer to death
means not increasing holiness
but a dawning awareness of
being taken out of time.'
SISTER JANE,
LOVING GOD WHATEVER
FAIRACRES PUBLICATIONS 155

Faith is trusting that
everything coming to you
out of the future
will work out well,
for your greater well-being.

'To live in this world
you must be able
to do three things:
to love what is mortal;
to hold it
against your bones knowing
your life depends on it;
and when the time comes to let it go,
to let it go.'
MARY OLIVER
'IN BLACKWATER WOODS'

This is the hour of lead
Remembered, if outlived,
As freezing persons recollect the snow,
first chill, then stupor then the letting go.
EMILY DICKINSON
'AFTER GREAT PAIN, A FORMAL FEELING COMES'

JIM@COTTERCAIRNS.CO.UK

WWW.COTTERCAIRNS.CO.UK

WWW.ST-HYWYN.ORG.UK

MARION GRAY

More than just another day

'Tomorrow never comes,' they say, and yet sometimes it comes all too soon. We look forward to what the future may hold, in equal measures of eager expectation as we anticipate a treat, and fear as we dread the worst. Tomorrow, of course, may never come. None of us knows when the end will come, only God, and he ain't telling—with good reason.

author

Marion Gray is a Reader in the Diocese of Southwark. She is Director of Reader Selection for the diocese and teaches on the Reader Training course.

Tomorrow is another day. It's the day when I'm going to start my new diet or my new exercise regime. It's the day for doing the things I could have done today but didn't need to. The anxieties I take to bed with me will seem much less important tomorrow morning. Tomorrow is somehow a long way off. The writer of Proverbs says, 'Do not boast about tomorrow, for you do not know what a day may bring' (27:1, NRSV). We may think we know what is coming, but there is no inevitability. We have to accept that there is nothing fixed about the future until it becomes the present.

Our attitude to the future is ambivalent. We make plans which reassure us that everything has been thought through, all the options considered, nothing left to chance. What could possibly go wrong? And yet we know all about the 'best-laid plans', so why are we surprised when things don't turn out as they were supposed to? Plans don't make things happen: my plan to write this article today only happened when I got on and did it.

We need to remember that the future belongs to God

We are to live in the present

We can very easily plan too much and have expectations that cannot be fulfilled. We need to remember that the future belongs to God, and, whether or not we believe he has everything mapped out in advance, we do ourselves no favours by holding rigid views of what ought to be happening. Jesus said, 'Do not worry about tomorrow, for tomorrow will bring worries of its own' (Matthew 6:34). He didn't mean that we should live without thinking ahead: the Authorised Version's 'take no thought for the morrow' seems to overstate the case, as it would be foolish (perhaps like building our house on the sand) not to look ahead in some respects—with regard to pensions, qualifications and relationships. However, we cannot let concern about material things displace our dependence on the Holy Spirit to guide us in every aspect of our lives. Jesus urges us not to *worry* about such things. No amount of worrying adds to the pension plan, any more than it can make you live longer (Matthew 6:27).

The message is that the future is God's concern. We are to live in the present, remaining open to the future, neither driven by fear nor holding on to false hopes that must necessarily be dashed. We can take assurance from the words in Jeremiah 29:11: 'For surely I know the plans I have for you, says the Lord, plans for your welfare and not for harm, to give you a future with hope. The key word here is 'hope', and it is very important to remember that the hope God gives us is a sure and certain hope based on his faithfulness and his promises—promises that can never fail (see 1 Kings 8:56).

What God has not promised is that everything will be just as we want it; nor has he promised that things won't appear to go wrong, at least from our perspective. It is obvious from looking at the world around us that God's will is often hindered or obstructed by the things people do. But God's will is for the whole of creation to be reconciled to him and transformed so that it can share fully in his limitless life—and God's will, in the end, will prevail. Because we know that God is a God of love, we know that love and goodness are the marks of the coming kingdom.

Many people argue that God knows everything that is going to happen. Because God is omniscient, he must know the future; otherwise his knowledge would be limited. God transcends time, and this means that he is outside our time, in the position of an observer who can see all the time that will ever exist—rather like someone perched on a mountain top who can see everything in the valley below. This was the way Thomas Aquinas described God's relationship to time. It means that God is just as close to the beginning as to the end of time, and to every point in between. He knows exactly what is going to happen in the future because, in a sense, to him it already exists.

That view presents us with a problem, though. God is omniscient and his knowledge must be perfect. So if God knows that something will happen in the future—for example, that next Tuesday I am going to buy a new laptop—then it must happen. I cannot decide not to buy a new laptop next Tuesday. But what about my free will? Was it a free decision to purchase a

> The hope God gives us is a sure and certain hope based on his faithfulness and his promises…

new laptop or was my decision already determined by God's foreknowledge of my action? There are various ways in which this argument can be developed, and philosophers are divided as to the correct answer. Some would say that although, in one sense, God knows what I would do, what he actually knows is that I will freely choose to buy the laptop. That is one approach to the problem. A simpler approach is to argue that the future does not exist and so God cannot know what will happen (a position known as 'open theism'). This does not threaten his omniscience as there is nothing for him to know. While God knows everything that has happened, he has no knowledge of future events, only of their possibility.

God's plans as mentioned in Jeremiah are not determinative any more than our plans are: God wills for certain things to happen, but that does not mean that they will happen. Put it another way: God does not will for evil things to happen, but they do.

John Polkinghorne, who was an eminent scientist before becoming a priest, has written extensively about God and science, including the relationship between God and time. He writes this:

Open theology pictures God as in providential interaction with divinely ordained natural processes and with the divinely allowed acts of free agents. On this view, the history of the universe is understood to resemble an unfolding improvisation in which the Creator is ceaselessly at work to bring about a harmonious resolution of the great multi-part fugue of creation.

THEOLOGY IN THE CONTEXT OF SCIENCE (SPCK, 2008)

So we see every present moment arising as the outcome of all that already is, but under the guiding hand of the Creator. There is no already-existing unfilled lump of time called the future: the only thing existing ahead of the present moment is God. The present unfolds from the past and, as God has created everything to exist freely and independent from him, so things can turn out differently from the way we might expect or wish.

The present unfolds not in a haphazard way but in ways that are contingent upon what has already happened. Just as, in a piece of improvised music, there is always scope to change key or go off at a tangent from the main theme, so in evolution, for example, mutations occur that can lead to a new species. This is God's creative power at work. Suffering and evil are the price we pay for our freedom and independence, and the freedom of the created universe to develop as it has done from the beginning.

God can and does work where there is openness: that is what prayer is about. In prayer we make ourselves open to the working of the Holy Spirit. Wherever there is openness, then God, through the working of the Holy Spirit, can influence what happens. In the non-

In prayer we make ourselves open to the working of the Holy Spirit

human creation, openness arises when the probability of a number of different outcomes is equally likely, so there is no strong determining influence.

> ## We cannot hope to have any influence in the future if we are not doing something today

Those are my reasons for believing that tomorrow doesn't exist, and that there is nothing I can do to make it happen. But I can be prepared, and I might be able to influence what happens. No self-respecting athlete goes into a race unprepared: there are training and practice as well as the basic skill and talent. Paul tells us to be like athletes training ourselves for the Christian life (1 Corinthians 9:24–27): we need to be disciplined and work hard at putting our faith into practice. The more we read our Bibles, spend time in prayer and live close to God, developing the skill of listening to him and for him, the better prepared we are to make God's love real to the people around us. As we pray, we are cooperating with God to bring about his will on earth, working with him to build the present and influence what can happen next.

Just as too much planning tends to close off possibilities for the future, if our lives are too laid back, if mañana will do, then we are not open to God and we are not available to him to help bring about his will. Jesus warned us not to worry about the future, but he also encouraged his listeners to think ahead and count the cost (Luke 14:28), to build on the rock, not on the sand (Matthew 7:24–26), to seek heavenly treasure (6:20–21), to forgive past wrongs and to mend relationships (5:22–24). These are all things that make us fit for tomorrow. If we are burdened by our past, by the hurts we have suffered and by anxiety about the future, then we are not ready for the life God calls us to share in, the life of tomorrow, the coming kingdom of God.

Tomorrow is God's time. As God transcends and is beyond time, the unfolding present is his gift to us from his eternity. As gift, it is freely given, which means that what will happen is not determined in advance. God does not send us bad things or make bad things happen, but he does not forcibly intervene to stop us doing the wrong thing if we are not listening to him. It is only human beings who can take action to relieve suffering, bring an end to poverty and injustice, and stop the overuse of the natural resources of the earth. In the words of Teresa of Avila, God has no hands but ours, and he depends on people to do his will—and they can be any people, not just Christians. This active doing of God's will has to be done today if it is to have any influence on what might happen tomorrow. We cannot hope to have any influence in the future if we are not doing something today.

Without God, tomorrow is a chimera. With God, we live today so that we can leave tomorrow to him. That is the Bible's message, as well as the message from the scientists who are warning us about climate change. We cannot live like the Israelites in Isaiah's time, who ignored the prophet's call to repentance: 'Let us eat and drink, for tomorrow we die,' they said (Isaiah 22:13). We cannot live selfishly, without regard for coming generations. We are stewards of God's creation and are called to husband and shepherd its fruitfulness for the sake of all people, not just ourselves. In that sense, tomorrow is very important and we ignore the call at our peril. Life in God's world is based on God's justice, and that includes justice for future generations.

Tomorrow is the time of God's kingdom— the time when God will reign and be known as Lord of all creation, when every knee will bow and God's loving purposes for creation will be fulfilled. The day will come—of that we can be sure—and it will be the end of time as we know it. We look forward to it with eager anticipation, and we pray for its coming. The unending and limitless life that God offers us in Jesus starts today, not tomorrow. Tomorrow is God's time and, as we share in Jesus' risen life by the power of the Spirit, we make that tomorrow kind of life a present reality.

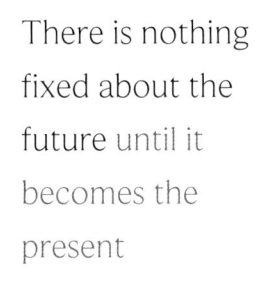

There is nothing fixed about the future until it becomes the present

DAVID SPRIGGS

Beyond tomorrow

> ... knowledge of the past

We have looked back to yesterday, explored today and, in this issue, have imagined our tomorrows. But what about 'beyond tomorrow'? Tomorrow is essentially a projection of yesterday and today into the future. Although we

author

David Spriggs is a Baptist minister who currently works for Bible Society. He has written a number of books.

are warned against being presumptuous about tomorrow (James 4:13–15), we can only plan and prepare because we can imagine it on the basis of our knowledge of the past. Inevitably, this process, so important for humans, makes assumptions about continuity— that time will continue, that some of the laws of nature will still operate, that certain resources will be available to us, that logic will still apply and even that changes will continue to happen.

'Beyond tomorrow' represents the boundary that prohibits the automatic validity of such speculations. It supposes a reality that is impervious to our ordinary projections. How shall we handle this idea?

We can deny its possibility, believing that there is no 'beyond tomorrow'

It supposes a reality that is impervious to **our ordinary projections**

One of the great passages of scripture that draw us 'beyond tomorrow' is to be found in Revelation 21–22. The current Bishop of Durham calls it 'perhaps the greatest image of new creation' (Tom Wright, *Surprised by Hope*, SPCK, 2007, p. 115). We will focus our reflections on the opening five verses of chapter 22:

The angel showed me a river that was crystal clear, and its waters gave life. The river came from the throne where God and the Lamb were seated. Then it flowed down the middle of the city's main street. On each side of the river are trees that grow a different kind of fruit each month of the year. The fruit gives life, and the

> To consider that there could be a 'beyond tomorrow' is itself a **gracious gift of God**

as there will always be another 'tomorrow'—but to do this is to deny the freedom of God. We can claim complete agnosticism: tomorrow cannot be known. The only proper human response to this is to discipline ourselves to avoid speculating. Or we can recognise that while we cannot construct tomorrow by ourselves, insights concerning it can be given to us by revelation from God. Indeed, unless our yearning to see 'beyond tomorrow' is understood as part of our fallen nature (eating of the fruit of the tree of knowledge, perhaps: see Genesis 2:17), then our ability to consider that there could be a 'beyond tomorrow' is itself a gracious gift of God. As God has provided insights for us, this, it seems to me, is the proper way to respond.

leaves are used as medicine to heal the nations. God's curse will no longer be on the people of that city. He and the Lamb will be seated there on their thrones, and its people will worship God and will see him face to face. God's name will be written on the foreheads of the people. Never again will night appear, and no one who lives there will ever need a lamp or the sun. The Lord God will be their light, and they will rule forever (CEV).

> We are drawn into the artist's world…

Works of art

I am fascinated by those TV programmes that take a well-known work of art, a sculpture such as Rodin's *The Kiss* or a painting such as Goya's *The Third of May*, and provide us with insights which only a finely attuned eye, informed with deep study and historical awareness, can bring. Something we already valued, maybe loved, now has greater depth. If we did not already find something beautiful or fascinating in the art, then we would probably not make the journey with the scholar to discover more, but we are enriched by doing so.

Many of us may have been drawn into the art of Jan Vermeer through the 2003 film, based on the book by Tracy Chevalier, *Girl with a Pearl Earring*. This painting has many of the 'hallmark' characteristics of Vermeer—his ability to communicate textures and colours, the fascination with light and darkness, the stillness of the scene, the composure of the subject, but perhaps above all the invitation of the eyes, which draw us into the life of the person depicted.

Like his other works, such as *Woman holding a Balance*, the composition and the execution warrant our full attention. The scenes are so exquisitely portrayed that we are drawn into the artist's world. We certainly sense that we could feel the different fabrics, catch the mood of the subject, feel the warmth of the sun and, if we allow ourselves, construct a relationship with the person before us and imagine their lives—at least a little. The richness of the painting is such that it requests us to stay, linger and live in it. It is powerful art.

Guided by the experts, however, we soon discover that there is far more in these paintings than we grasp at first. They point out that the picture behind the woman with the balance is of the Last Judgment, so the balances, as well as being instruments for weighing the jewellery and establishing its value, also symbolise the need to weigh the pursuit of wealth against moral and spiritual goods. If, as some suggest, the woman in the picture is pregnant, this need becomes even more pointed. Then, if we recall the financial challenges that Vermeer himself constantly faced, a more pressing and intimate dimension is brought in as well.

So we can appreciate this picture at two levels—the immediate, where we take it for what it is on the surface, and the informed, where new levels of engagement take place because we are studying the picture in more depth.

Both the immediate and informed viewings are valid and enriching. The immediate view engages our imagination: the art stimulates our sensitivities and helps us enter a different world. The informed view offers us the insights of decades of intense scholarship

Something **beautiful** or fascinating in the art...

and investigation so as to deepen the meaning that we find in the picture.

Revelation 21—22 can work for us similarly as we seek to appreciate and respond to the insights that God offers us 'beyond tomorrow'.

> It leads our eye to its source, and so we find ourselves before **the throne of God and of the Lamb**

Imagination: seeing with ordinary eyes

How do you see the picture presented to us in Revelation 22:1—5? Please read this passage as slowly as you can without losing the totality—perhaps pausing to take a deep breath after each phrase. Having done this, more than once if you wish, what do you see, sense, hear, smell and feel? If you were an artist, how would you compose a picture of the scene? What style might you use in order to convey this vision? Will the whole

canvas focus on the scene as described? Will you include, in some way, John being shown the vision by an angel? If so, how will the angel 'show him': does he point it out, does he remove scales from John's eyes or does he conjure the vision up inside his head?

What of the scene itself? Running through it is a river. This is the visual thread around which the scene coheres. It leads our eye to its source, and so we find ourselves before the throne of God and of the Lamb. Indeed, they are the centre point of the picture. We are awestruck by their glory and grace. As we attend to them, we see that they are surrounded by the servants who worship, gazing in adoration, enlivened by their personal engagement with God. We linger with them and catch the mystery and privilege that is theirs.

Then our eyes are drawn away by the shimmering of the river. It is so well painted that we seem to be borne along with it, cascading through the picture. We see that this river, although crystal pure and meandering, is part of a city—a beautiful city, a peaceful city, yet a vibrant place. Perhaps, as if it were some Venetian scene, we long to explore its riches and mystery, to sample its food, share in its conversations, admire its creativity, enjoy its music… yet the picture insists that we look again, for there is a glorious tree in it. What colour is appropriate for leaves with such a moving purpose? For now, I must leave you to complete your picture…

There is so much to engage with, as a picture is constructed through the words. For me, although it is vibrant with purpose and dynamic, the scene is also restful and refreshing. In the end, the dominance of God's presence is balanced by the tree of life for the healing of the nations, linked by this amazing stream, full of light and life. 'Beyond tomorrow' is filled for me with the joyous presence of God, the communion of saints and the restoration of all the nations to the purposes of God. Life and human history have not been lost but now, at last, have been fulfilled.

Investigation: through other eyes

What can be added by the informed minds of those who study this passage? We might select just one component— the river. If we are to deepen our appreciation of this river, we need to recall at least four Old Testament texts.

Psalm 46 begins with the sense of God providing absolute security for his people, even if cosmic upheavals are taking place (vv. 1–3), and the symbol for this security is a river: 'There is a river that brings joy to the city of God, to the sacred house of the Most High. God is in that city' (vv. 4–5a, GNB). Of course, rivers were not a prominent part of Jerusalem's geography. Huge efforts had to be made to ensure an adequate water supply, particularly in time of siege. So already, in this psalm, the 'river' is a big advance on the 'real' Jerusalem. It is a rich symbol of God's presence and the abundance of life that he provides.

Restful and refreshing…

It is a rich symbol of God's presence and the abundance of life that he provides…

The book of Ezekiel develops this river image as part of the 'new temple' in chapters 40–48. In 47:1–12 there is an amazing river. Its source is the heart of the temple, the altar, but this river is miraculous. As it flows, it gets deeper and broader, until it becomes immense. It flows through the land southwards towards the desert and the 'Dead Sea'. Wherever it flows, it brings fertility to the land, and the river itself teems with fish. It not only brings fertility but also replaces the salty waters with fresh (compare Exodus 17:1–7; 2 Kings

> There is nothing beyond this **new Jerusalem**

2:20–22). Here, too, we are introduced to 'all kinds' of trees, which never wither, produce fruit every month and whose leaves are for healing people (47:12).

Clearly, Ezekiel 47 is a major source for John's vision, but, just because of this, we need to note a couple of differences. First, John's river does not emerge from the altar and flow from the temple. It

cannot because there is no temple, let alone altar. Rather, this river is the 'real thing'. It flows from the throne of God; it is the stream of his presence. It proceeds from the Lamb, not the altar—not from the place where sacrifices were made on earth but from the real eternal sacrifice. Second, it does not flow out of the city to bring healing to the barren places. Is this, then, a more restricted vision than Ezekiel's? Certainly not: there is nothing beyond this new Jerusalem and there are no barren places. The new Jerusalem encompasses all that there is, in every dimension: it is described as a cube, not a square, and of a vast size (Revelation 21:16). At the very least, the river reminds us that 'beyond tomorrow' will be the fulfilment of all our worship— and that is the 'chief end of man'.

The third related Old Testament passage is Genesis 2:8–17, depicting the garden of Eden with its river and fruitful trees. This is an important source for both Ezekiel and Revelation. John is indicating that the new Jerusalem is the completion of God's original intentions for the created world. But it is more: it is an advance. It is a city (not simply a garden), and there is no longer the risk of disobedience: there is only one tree, the tree of life, even though it seems to stand on both sides of the river.

The final Old Testament passage that is echoed in Revelation 22:1–5 is from Psalm 1. In verse 3 of this psalm, the righteous are described as follows: 'They are like trees that grow beside a stream, that bear fruit at the right time, and whose leaves do not dry up. They succeed in everything they do' (GNB). This, I would suggest, indicates that the tree is another image for the Bride of Christ—the saints. So our role in the new Jerusalem will not be passive or restricted to playing harps! It will be to develop the city from one degree of perfection to another. We will continue to be fully engaged in the new mission of God—for the healing of the nations.

Recalling Old Testament passages is not the whole story, however. It seems highly probable to me that John's picture is also recalling Jesus' words in John 7:38–39. Here Jesus speaks of 'life-giving streams' flowing from his side, and decodes the stream as 'the Spirit'. This indicates that John is thinking in trinitarian terms, even though he only specifically mentions the 'One on the throne' and the Lamb.

> … an enriched version of anything we have experienced on earth

Conclusion

As we explore some of the depths behind this passage, we can see how the intentions of God, the glimpsed experiences of God's people and the daring vision of the prophet are gathered together seamlessly within John's portrayal. This indicates that, beyond tomorrow, the new Jerusalem is a real place, but also an enriched version of anything we have experienced on earth. It is, as is everything and everyone there, bathed in the embracing presence of God. But within this picture is a dynamic and fulfilling life for all who 'have washed their robes in the blood of the lamb' (Revelation 7:14, CEV). While we cannot, of ourselves, see beyond tomorrow, through the eyes of this revelation we can feel the powerful magnetism of God's new future.

INFORMATION ABOUT THE PAINTINGS MENTIONED CAN BE FOUND IN WIKIPEDIA, THE FREE INTERNET ENCYCLOPEDIA.

My Space

This space is for you to make your own notes.

On the beach, waiting for the tide to turn

© Heather Fenton 2008

Psalm 16

My full cup of blessing, my gift for the future,
Lord, you, and you only, hold my life secure.
The tent of my life is spread out as you've chosen
The place of your choosing, delightful and sure.
By night in the silence I hear your instruction,
And deep in my heart I respond to your call.
God, always before me, within and without me,
With you at my right hand I never shall fall.

So my heart exults and my soul is rejoicing,
My body in safety will rest and be free.
For you'll not abandon my soul to the darkness
But on your sure pathway my journey shall be.
In your sweetest presence is joy without measure,
Eternally welling, unbounded and true;
And at your right hand are the truest of pleasures.
With all of my heart I'll be faithful to you.

Despair and hope:

a meditation for a small group

Then I saw a new heaven and a new earth, for the first heaven and the first earth had passed away.

REVELATION 21:1A (NIV)

Our world is fraught

author

Heather Fenton works as a parish priest and editor of *The Reader* magazine.

Arrange some rubbish in the centre of the group—a few old cans, maybe, a supermarket bag, a picture of a tip, an empty food packet. The words in italic type are those which all the group members say together.

Leader: Today our world is fraught with so many problems. We label them to help us feel we have some control. We use words such as 'environmental damage', 'climate change', 'global warming', 'carbon offsets'. We hear talk of how the world will be in the future— the broken world we may leave to our children and grandchildren. We stand on the edge of disaster.

> In spite of the
> destruction, we have
> discovered so many
> **wonderful things**

All: *Lord, we grieve for your world. Forgive us because we have ignored the warning signs for so long. Lord, in your mercy: hear our prayer.*

Leader: Our world is so wonderful, Lord, so diverse. In our own generation, in spite of the destruction, we have discovered so many wonderful things. 'All things bright and beautiful,' we sang as children. But will our children and grandchildren see these things, or will they be merely pictures on a website, illustrating a lost world?

All: *Lord, we grieve for your world. Forgive us because we have ignored the warning signs for so long. Lord, in your mercy: hear our prayer.*

Leader: Our people are so fragile, Lord. Our families and nations are undermined by debt. Relationships

are torn apart by poverty, drugs and homelessness. We are powerless to help ourselves.

All: *Lord, we grieve for your world. Forgive us because we have ignored the warning signs for so long. Lord, in your mercy: hear our prayer.*

Leader: Lord, we go to the supermarket and see shelves still packed with goods from here, there and everywhere. Yet the world grows hungrier daily, and still we do not understand the plight of others or the dangers we face ourselves.

> Lord, in your mercy:
> **hear our prayer**

All: *Lord, we grieve for your world. Forgive us because we have ignored the warning signs for so long. Lord, in your mercy: hear our prayer.*

Place a glass of water on the table.

Leader: John, in the book of Revelation, speaks of living water like this: 'Then the angel showed me the river of the water of life, as clear as crystal, flowing from the throne of God and of the Lamb down the middle of the great street of the city. On each side of the river stood the tree of life, bearing twelve crops of fruit, yielding its fruit every month. And the leaves of the tree are for the healing of the nations. No longer will there be any curse. The throne of God and of the Lamb will be in the city, and his servants will serve him' (Revelation 22:1–3, NIV).

Enable us to be those who wait faithfully for your coming, living lives of prayer and discipline, faith and love

… your coming kingdom

All: Lord, we pray for our world. Enable us to put all our hope in you. Give to us your living water. Lord, in your mercy: hear our prayer.

Place some leaves or small branches on the table.

Leader: Lord, give us hope. May the nations of the world know the leaves of that tree, bringing them healing and life. May we, your people, wait with faithful expectation of your coming.

All: Lord, we pray for the nations of the world. May they receive with joy the healing you have prepared for them. Lord, in your mercy: hear our prayer.

Remove the rubbish that is with the water and the leaves and put it out of sight.

All: And as we wait, remove from us, Lord, the clutter we have in our own lives. Help us to be those who point to your coming kingdom. Enable us to be those who wait faithfully for your coming, living lives of prayer and discipline, faith and love. Those who, while waiting, pray: Our Father, which art in heaven…

SIMON BARRINGTON-WARD

A first encounter with the Jesus Prayer

This extract is taken from *The Jesus Prayer* by Simon Barrington-Ward (BRF, 2007). For further information, see www.brfonline.org.uk.

I came across the Jesus Prayer at a time when I was travelling in different parts of the world for the Church Missionary Society. It was those travels that made me hunger for a better way of praying, a way that would be more adequate to all that I was then encountering in Africa and Asia. Even on my return to this country I was becoming more aware than ever before of deep currents flowing in our own society.

Sometimes I could sense, underlying so many casual meetings and conversations across the globe, so many glimpses of the way people were living and striving and suffering—glimpses snatched even as I cycled into London, even around our offices in Waterloo—some kind of universal struggle. There seemed to be so many contradictions at every level in my life and in the whole

author

Simon Barrington-Ward, a former Bishop of Coventry, now travels widely, speaking on prayer and spirituality and the Jesus Prayer in particular.

of human society. There seemed to be, underlying everything, some kind of vast, inchoate yearning, which I could also feel, more and more of the time, in my own heart and which seemed to be increasingly present in everything I was trying to do.

Gradually it focused on a longing for a real deepening of prayer—and of the whole of my 'life in Christ'. I was thirsting for something that was more universal, deeper, wider than my previous attempts at prayer. I was thirsting for a way of praying that genuinely embraced all the people and situations that still cried out to me when I paused for a moment, and yet at the same time came to grips more realistically with the frustrations and longings of my own divided nature.

One day a friend took me down to a Russian Orthodox monastery in Essex. It was just a small monastery, with both monks and sisters. (This happened some years ago, and before that I had never had very much to do with the Orthodox Church.)

As soon as we arrived, we both went straight into the chapel, because the community and their guests were starting their evening Office. I imagined it was going to be like the Offices in most monasteries in the West, with some kind of traditional form like that of our own morning and evening prayer, which, after all, came out of the monastic tradition.

But instead they had something quite different. There was just one voice leading what has long been called the Jesus Prayer—a woman's voice—and the others were praying it silently with her.

> There was a pause. Then the prayer was repeated

We stood there in the darkened chapel, with all the icons and screens around, and little lights burning. I was conscious of the shapes of the brothers and sisters around me and of their faces—faces as striking as that of Father Sophrony, a remarkable bearded countenance with a great quality of shrewdness and humour and also radiance about it, absorbed in the gentle flow of the prayer.

It was as if the faces of the brothers and sisters around me were somehow merging into the faces on the icons all round the walls, and I was conscious of how very easily you could find yourself one with them as the generations

slipped back and back.

There was an icon of St Silouan, the person from whom Father Sophrony had learnt about the Jesus Prayer. I had seen Silouan's face in a photograph on the back of Father Sophrony's book about him; and now, there he was, in an icon—which Father Sophrony told me later was a much better likeness of him than the photograph. The photograph was too sombre, with his heavy eyebrows, dark gaze and massive beard dominating. The icon showed the real lightness and the gleam of response which were also always there.

Through the rows of smaller icons we went back to the next generation, and back through the years to St Seraphim of Sarov, with his white hair and beard and his white robe, bowed with frailty but shining and alive with joy and risen life; then to all the great Russian saints before him and, before them, reaching back to the Byzantine and Eastern Fathers and Mothers, to the Desert Saints, and, at the heart of all, the apostles and John the Baptist, after whom the monastery was named—back to the Evangelists, to St John and to the Virgin Mary and to the whole Gospel story. Beyond us and over us was the Last Supper and above us the vision of God in heaven. It all seemed of a piece, as if we were all going forward together in this one great community in time and space and eternity.

That was the setting in which I first met the Jesus Prayer, and that whole setting was very important, because the prayer was already being said when we went into the chapel. The prayer was spoken mostly in English, because much of their liturgy is in English, but there were short stretches of time in which it was spoken in Greek and also in Russian. A sister who was leading at first handed over to a monk after a while, simply praying:

'Lord Jesus Christ, Son of God, have mercy on me.'

There was a pause. Then the prayer was repeated. We were lifted up into the steady wingbeat of the prayer. As we settled into it and began to be drawn into it, we felt that it became the focal theme of the whole community and of our own being.

One's mind could wander—and we could even go to sleep (especially if we had kindly been given a chair to sit in, as I had). Yet all the time the prayer was going on, and we were part of it. Indeed, the constant re-emphasis of the words 'Lord Jesus Christ' kept on recalling me to the presence, and the constant movement of the prayer, 'Have mercy

on me', immediately began to grasp me very deeply. After I came out of the chapel, the prayer was still praying itself inside me for many hours.

Later, I talked with Father Sophrony, and from that first occasion on we talked many times. He became a helper to me and a spiritual guide. He has since slipped through the veil—which in his presence always seemed so thin—that

> After I came out of the chapel, the prayer was still praying itself inside me for many hours

separates us still from that radiant host on the chapel wall. But, like the rest, he is still close to us. His shrewd twinkling gaze still looks at me from a photograph on my study wall, peering quizzically across at me as he always did, as if he were humorously and affectionately aware of all my evasions and yet always ready to guide me beyond them. In this prayer particularly, I think we need that sort of help.

LIZ PACEY

Liz's prayers

Jesus Christ is the same yesterday and today and for ever.
HEBREWS 13:8

Please help me to
get my priorities right

Tomorrow. It lies open before us, a vast expanse of… what? Is it something we dread, or embrace with open arms? Or something we take as it comes? Find a quiet place, a place where you can comfortably relax, and open your heart and mind to the God of yesterday, today and for ever. What is he saying to you?

Now listen, you who say, 'Today or tomorrow we will go to this or that city, spend a year there, carry on business and make money.'
JAMES 4:13

Is this me, Lord? I'm a great one for making plans, and I don't always think about making time and space to find out if I'm on your track. My diary is a magnet, attracting more tasks than I can ever fit into a day. Do I put business and money before knowing your will for my life? Please help me to get my priorities right.

Why, you do not even know what will happen tomorrow. What is your life? You are a mist that appears for a little while and then vanishes.
JAMES 4:14

author

Liz Pacey is a Reader in the Church of England, freelance writer and a mature theology and ministry student.

Sometimes my life seems shallow and I feel tossed about from pillar to post. I wonder whether, when I vanish from this life, I will leave anything worthwhile behind. I wonder about the people around me and what impact my life has had and will have on them.

I pray for tomorrow, that whether or not it seems like an important day,

> I pray for tomorrow

Whenever the rainbow appears in the clouds, I will see it and remember the everlasting covenant...

whatever it brings, whether good or bad, I will shine as a beacon for you.

'For I know the plans I have for you,' declares the Lord, 'plans to prosper you and not to harm you, plans to give you hope and a future.'
JEREMIAH 29: 11

Wow, Lord! This puts a different complexion on things. You've got plans for me. When things are going well, I can thank you for your hand on my life. Then, when things aren't going to my plan, I will see that better things are in store. I'll hear you say, 'Trust me. I'll get you through. I have plans for you.'

I'll learn to hold my plans lightly in my hands, be ready to be surprised by you and allow space in my life for the unlikely and the extraordinary.

'Whenever the rainbow appears in the clouds, I will see it and remember the everlasting covenant between God and all living creatures of every kind on the earth.'
GENESIS 9:16

Sometimes, Lord, I think you must despair of me—the times when all I can see is the clouds, and can't imagine that there could be anything beyond.

Then there are the times when I think my head is too far in the clouds. Like a child excitedly waiting for Christmas, I'm so busy trying to reach tomorrow that I don't have time to appreciate today.

I need to learn to live in the present but be open to the future. Thank you for the rainbow, which reminds me of my tomorrow with you.

I'm so busy trying to reach tomorrow that **I don't have time to appreciate today**

'Therefore do not worry about tomorrow, for tomorrow will worry about itself. Each day has enough trouble of its own.'
MATTHEW 6:34

'Don't worry about tomorrow.' That's all very well for you to say, God. You know what's going to happen tomorrow, but I don't. How can I trust that all will be well? Is my tomorrow all mapped out? Don't I have any say?

No, I can't believe that, Lord. You love me too much for that. You don't want me sitting around waiting for things to happen. You want me working alongside you.

Meditation

Lord, I'm looking outside as the rain falls. I notice how a single drop ripples out into a little pool, and that pool runs into another; then more pools join, and more, and soon there is a flowing river.

I feel like that little single raindrop sometimes, small and very insignificant, but every now and again you let me see the larger picture, and I realise that I am one in a company of many. Together we can work to change things for the better for the future.

'Your kingdom come, your will be done on earth as it is in heaven.'
MATTHEW 6:10

We look for the coming of your kingdom in the future, but we have to live it today, too.

Help me to be positive about tomorrow, to visualise the good in it, whatever my circumstances now. Help me to be careful in the choices I make, which affect not only my tomorrow but that of others. Don't let my mistakes mar the future. Enable me to forgive and forget and not carry grudges forward.

'In my Father's house are many rooms; if it were not so, I would have told you. I am going there to prepare a place for you.'
JOHN 14:2

Lord, thank you that we have your promise that you have gone ahead to prepare a place for us.
We thank you, too, for the places that bring us close to you here on earth. Sometimes we have to look back to go forward. We thank you for our holy

Sometimes we have to look back to go forward

Tomorrow is a gift...

places, where we feel not only that we are touching heaven but also that we are touching the lives of the saints down the ages. We are pilgrims together as we journey towards our tomorrow.

Then the angel showed me the river of the water of life, as clear as crystal, flowing down from the throne of God and of the Lamb.
REVELATION 22:1

You give us such vivid pictures of what heaven is going to be like; it is far beyond my earthly imagination. As a caterpillar can't possibly imagine what it is like to become a butterfly, I can't really imagine what life beyond tomorrow will be like. But I read about it in your word, and I long for it.

Surely goodness and love will follow me all the days of my life, and I will dwell in the house of the Lord for ever.
PSALM 23:6

Tomorrow is a gift from you, Lord, and we give it back to you. As we live out our ordinary lives, may we have our eyes on the extraordinary, the wonderful tomorrow that we will have in your kingdom.

ALL BIBLE REFERENCES ARE TAKEN FROM THE NEW INTERNATIONAL VERSION OF THE BIBLE.

My Prayers

This space is for you to make your own notes.

On the beach, waiting for the tide to turn

© *Heather Fenton 2008*

Tomorrow is another day

Some years ago, a political party in Britain used the slogan 'A better tomorrow'. A cartoonist drew a picture of party activists proclaiming their message, and underneath were the words, 'And when tomorrow comes, they'll say "Tomorrow".'

author

Tony Horsfall is a freelance trainer and retreat leader living in Yorkshire. He is the author of *Mentoring for Spiritual Growth* (2008) and *Working from a Place of Rest* (2010), both published by BRF.

The fickle nature of political promises is well known, but thoughts about tomorrow are inevitable, and the way we consider the future can significantly affect the way we live today.

Sometimes we feel *anxious* about tomorrow.

The future is unknown and unpredictable, and can be frightening. Perhaps today, as you read these words, you are nervous about what lies ahead. It might be that you are waiting for the results of a hospital test… facing a tough exam at school or college… planning a visit to the dentist… anticipating a difficult meeting… wondering how you will pay the bills… feeling you just can't make that deadline… worrying about your children or loved ones… thinking

The future is
unknown and
unpredictable, and
can be frightening

Negative thoughts about the future have to be counteracted by positive thoughts about the Father's watchfulness

Feeling anxious is normal

about an unwelcome change ahead of you.

Feeling anxious is normal, and anticipating what lies ahead is part of how we prepare ourselves to cope with challenging situations. We all know, though, that excessive worrying about the future can be paralysing and can rob us of joy in the present moment.

If left unchecked, it can intensify into sinful unbelief and a failure to trust God with the details of our lives.

It was this negative outcome that Jesus sought to correct when he spoke to his disciples, reminding them of their heavenly Father's concern for them: 'Therefore do not worry about tomorrow, for tomorrow will worry about itself. Each day has enough trouble of its own' (Matthew 6:34, NIV). He urged them to remember the love and care that the Father takes over the created order (the birds, the flowers) and to know that his concern for them is even greater.

Negative thoughts about the future have to be counteracted by positive thoughts about the Father's watchfulness. 'Perfect love drives out fear,' says John (1 John 4:18), because the more we know ourselves to be loved by God, the more we will be able to live securely and overcome our fears.

What makes you anxious about tomorrow? Take some time to rest in the Father's love.

Meditate on these words:

Do you think anyone is going to be able to drive a wedge between us and Christ's love for us? There is no way! Not trouble, not hard times, not hatred, not hunger, not homelessness, not bullying threats, not backstabbing, not even the worst sins listed in Scripture... I'm absolutely convinced that nothing—nothing living or dead, angelic or demonic, today or tomorrow, high or low, thinkable or unthinkable—absolutely nothing can get between us and God's love because of the way that Jesus our Master has embraced us.

ROMANS 8:35, 38–39 (*THE MESSAGE*)

Sometimes we feel *excited* about tomorrow.

Maybe you are looking forward to the future. Perhaps you are anticipating a wedding, the birth of a child, a family celebration... looking forward to a much-needed holiday... starting a new job or moving house... getting paid at last... reaching retirement age... doing something you have always wanted to do.

The future opens up new possibilities, and we can allow our minds to imagine what could be, what might be. We can ask ourselves, 'What if...?' and dare to dream our dreams. We can allow God to fill our hearts with his vision for his kingdom, for his church and for our lives.

It is God who has given us such creative energy, and his Spirit plants the seeds of the future in our hearts. Isaiah

reminds God's people in exile that they still have a future. 'See, the former things have taken place,' he says, 'and new things I declare; before they spring into being I announce them to you' (Isaiah 42:9). The faithfulness of God in the past gives confidence for our vision of the future.

The future opens up new possibilities, and we can allow our minds to imagine what could be, what might be

Turn your excitement about the future into praise and thanksgiving. Take some time to dream. What God-given ideas are you holding? What might God be bringing to birth through you?

Meditate on these words:

Now to him who is able to do immeasurably more than all we ask or imagine, according to his power that is at work within us, to him be glory in the church and in Christ Jesus throughout all generations, for ever and ever! Amen.

EPHESIANS 3:20–21

Whether we are anxious or excited by the thought of tomorrow, all of us should feel *humble* as we think about the future.

The reality is that we do not know what the future holds. It is easy for us to make our plans, outline our strategies and set our goals, but life is full of unexpected events that we can never anticipate, that throw the best-laid plans into confusion. We like to be in control but we are not.

The apostle James gives us a reality check: 'Now listen, you who say, "Today or tomorrow we will go to this or that city, spend a year there, carry on business and make money." Why, you do not even know what will happen tomorrow. What is your life? You are a mist that appears for a little while and then vanishes. Instead, you ought to say, "If it is the Lord's will, we will live and do this or that"' (James 4:13–15).

Early in 2010, a volcanic eruption in Iceland brought air travel in Europe to a standstill. Insurers call such an event an 'act of God', and it certainly was a humbling reminder that even today's technological society can be brought to its knees by an unexpected event thousands of miles away. We need to avoid the pride-filled confidence that makes plans without dependence upon God. We may plan our way, but God directs our steps (Proverbs 16:9).

Think about times when your plans have been thrown into chaos. What can you learn from such events? How do these thoughts shape your future planning?

Meditate on these words:

'Do not boast about tomorrow, for you do not know what a day may bring forth.'

PROVERBS 27:1

> # Life is full of unexpected events that we can never anticipate, that throw the best-laid plans into confusion

Today I heard the small beginnings
Of a new tune.
Just a few notes
Drifting unexpectedly on the wind.
I should like to hear
The rest of the tune.
I should like to hear the harmonies
And see the pattern.
HEATHER FENTON

Deep peace of the running wave to you,
Deep peace of the flowing air to you,
Deep peace of the quiet earth to you,
Deep peace of the shining stars to you,
Deep peace of the Son of Peace to you, for ever.
SOURCE UNKNOWN (EARLY SCOTTISH)

St David's last words to the monks of the monastery which
he founded were 'Keep the faith and do the little things well.'

Keep the faith *and do little things well*

Margaret's Space

Margaret Harvey is a retired priest in the Church in Wales. She has been running Coleg y Groes Retreat House. Margaret writes a regular column in *Quiet Spaces*.

Space and time...

Tomorrow... Two pictures are there in my memory. One is of my sister and myself as children, sitting in bed, arguing when we should have been going to sleep. We could argue about most things, but this time it was about 'tomorrow'. I can't remember now which side of the argument I took. We puzzled together about whether it could ever be 'tomorrow'. By the time we were in tomorrow, one of us insisted, it wasn't 'tomorrow' but 'today'. It was a very strange argument for under-tens to be having, but we persisted with it until our mother came and told us off for being awake.

I can still remember the sense of insecurity and uncertainty that settled over us as we argued. The future can sometimes have that effect. We can be sensible and prepare for it; sometimes we can look forward to it with anticipation; but it is still unknown and ultimately uncontrollable. The unknown can be very unsettling.

The other picture I recall is of a small church somewhere in Italy. I have never actually seen it, but, as I listened to a talk in the college chapel many years ago, the speaker described it so vividly that the picture has remained in my imagination ever since. The nave of the church, where the congregation would sit, had a ceiling painted green. It symbolised the earth, the place where we find ourselves now, our everyday life 'today', the journey along the radius of the circle. The ceiling of the chancel at the east end of the church was blue. It represented the immensity of space and time, the unknown, the future, 'tomorrow'. The speaker thought of it as the circumference of the circle. It spoke of our need for a further and wider view than the immediate concerns of the day.

Going for a walk in the hills with eyes firmly fixed on our feet may mean that we avoid falling over stones, but, if we don't look up to the horizon, we don't appreciate where we are in relation to our surroundings and it is easy to get lost. Sometimes, though, the immensity of the horizon and the unknown future can make us feel lost, too. At the east end of the church in Italy, above the altar, there is a small stained-glass window with the face of a man. Jesus enables the vastness of the circumference and the scariness of the future to move into focus. It is as if God twists the lens of a projector until the vague, unstable image on the screen turns into something we can see.

> If we don't look up to the horizon, we don't **appreciate where we are...**

When you have some quiet, picture the Italian church in your imagination. Spend some time in the green-ceilinged nave. Wherever you are in this journey along the radius of life's circle, acknowledge it to yourself and before God. If you want to, talk to him about it. Then, when you are ready, move on into the chancel with the blue of the horizon. What comes into your mind as you contemplate the future? Now turn to the Gospels and the face of a man in the window over the altar. Try reading some of the chapters that John sets between the last supper and the arrest of Jesus (John 13−17), where Jesus helps his disciples to face the future. Listen to what he says. Take a word, phrase or idea with you into the day's future.

Leaves and lilies:
two-minute meditation

'And why do you worry about clothes? See how the lilies of the field grow. They do not labour or spin. Yet I tell you that not even Solomon in all his splendour was dressed like one of these. If that is how God clothes the grass of the field, which is here today and tomorrow is thrown into the fire, will he not much more clothe you, O you of little faith? So do not worry, saying, "What shall we eat?" or "What shall we drink?" or "What shall we wear?" For the pagans run after all these things, and your heavenly Father knows that you need them. But seek first his kingdom and his righteousness, and all these things will be given to you as well. Therefore do not worry about tomorrow, for tomorrow will worry about itself. Each day has enough trouble of its own.'

MATTHEW 6:28–34 (NIV)

author

Heather Fenton works as a parish priest and editor of The Reader magazine.

Take two minutes out of your day and…

Find a leaf,
Any kind of leaf.
Get it from the salad box in the fridge,
A pot plant, a hedge or a garden.
Take the leaf and turn it over and over in your hand.
Look at the shape.
See the structure.
Observe the colour.
Feel the texture
And the weight.

Prayer

*God of detail, thank you
for the small things in your
creation. Thank you for all
the beauties I so easily miss.
Thank you for shapes, for
structures, for textures. Thank
you for the varieties of the colour
for plants great and small, common
and exotic. Help me to notice your
little things, and enjoy them with
you. Amen*

HEATHER FENTON

And after Christmas...

an idea for a quiet corner

Why not make a quiet corner to take you from **Epiphany to Candlemas?**

author

Heather Fenton works as a parish priest and editor of *The Reader* magazine.

These days, Christmas seems to end abruptly. No sooner have we celebrated Christmas Day when, the next moment, we are pressurised by the push to go to the sales, or even go to work to sell all these things at post-Christmas prices. In fact, there are at least twelve days of Christmas, as the partridge in the pear tree keeps telling us, culminating with Epiphany on 6 January. We can even extend our thoughts about the God-given events we celebrated so briefly until Candlemas on 2 February.

Why not make a quiet corner to take you from Epiphany to Candlemas? Start by finding a symbol of the wise men. This could be a picture from a

Christmas card, or maybe a paper crown from a cracker or a small decorative box to represent the gifts. Failing that, a star from your Christmas decorations would be fine.

These three men (we think there were three only because there are three gifts mentioned in Matthew 2:1–12) were probably what, these days, we would call scientists. There is speculation that they could have been from a Zoroastrian priestly caste. *Magi* is the plural of *magus,* meaning a member of a hereditary priestly class among the ancient Medes and Persians. Observing the skies was their speciality, and what they saw there amazed them. 'After Jesus was born in Bethlehem in Judea, during the time of King Herod, Magi from the east came to Jerusalem and asked, "Where is the one who has been born king of the Jews? We saw his star in the east and have come to worship him"' (Matthew 2:1–2, NIV).

Spend some time with this story. If you are good at imagining, you could imagine that you were there too. Think about what gifts you could have brought to the new king. What would you have given, and why? Maybe it would be something that seems trivial, or it may be something very important to you. Take time to think. Then find a token of it, or write a word on a piece of paper. Put it in your quiet corner with the token of the king's gifts. You may want to revisit the gifts for a few days, spending a few minutes at a time. Allow God to speak to you about what you are offering—and maybe what you would

> Gold is a gift for a king

> If you are good at imagining, you could imagine that you were there too...

prefer to withhold from him. If, like the kings, you are working as a group or with a partner, what are you offering together?

The wise men's gifts themselves—gold, frankincense and myrrh—were full of meaning. Gold is a gift for a king, a royal gift which acknowledged who this child, born in humble circumstances, really was. The outsiders had been led to see the truth. After you have grown into the idea of offering a gift particular to you, spend a few moments during each of the next few days thinking about this gift of gold. It may not have expressed who the giver was, but it was very appropriate for Jesus. It was a gift for a king, and it was also very practical.

If you have ever been out of work for any length of time, you will know how helpful a gift of any kind can be. I was once in this situation and had been wondering how to pay for a new pair of glasses. Imagine my thrill and amazement when a person I hardly knew found out and just gave me the money! Well, after the wise men's visit, Joseph, the breadwinner of the family, suddenly had to give up his small business and escape into Egypt. As it is unlikely that he would have brought his tools with him when he responded to Rome's demand to take part in the census, he would have needed some more if he was going to have a chance of making a living so far from home. So perhaps the gold was spent on travel, temporary accommodation and business set-up

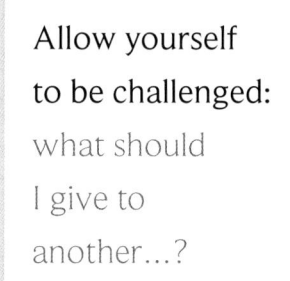

Allow yourself to be challenged: what should I give to another…?

costs. Who knows, but it is quite possible that this is what happened. Allow yourself to be challenged: what should I give to another, and what should I receive from another? Remember Romans 8:28: 'And we know that in all things God works for the good of those who love him, who have been called according to his purpose.'

Frankincense is not in everyday use for most of us! Not long ago, I saw a really interesting programme on the television. The presenter made an epic 2000-mile journey across the Middle East, following the ancient frankincense trade route from Arabia to the West. Frankincense, also called olibanum, is an aromatic resin (or dried sap) obtained from trees of the genus *Boswellia*. It is used in perfumes, so it would have made the stable smell sweeter. In Exodus 30:34, Aaron burnt it as a fragrant offering to the Lord, so symbolically it represents the divinity of Christ.

You could use a sweet-smelling candle, of frankincense or some other scent—to burn at your quiet corner.

Frankincense, also called olibanum, is an aromatic resin obtained from trees of the genus *Boswellia*

Frankincense is characterised by a balsamic-spicy, slightly lemony smell, with a conifer-like undertone. Writing to the Philippians, Paul talks about their response to the gospel in terms of 'a fragrant offering, an acceptable sacrifice, pleasing to God' (4:18). Who are the people to whom we can offer a response of thankfulness for bringing us, or helping us to understand better, the gospel of Christ?

What would you regret not having done or said to another if your death were to come sooner than you thought it would?

Take some time to think

Myrrh is also a sap, but it is bitter, not sweet like frankincense. It was less expensive but still highly valued, and was used mostly to embalm the dead. A practical use for Mary and Joseph would have been in medicine of some sort. Today it is used in items such as toothpaste, so, if you cannot find anything else to represent it in your quiet corner, you could try that!

Myrrh reminds us of Jesus' suffering. It makes us think, too, about the time when Jesus was anointed by Mary with expensive oil of nard, just before his suffering and death; and Nicodemus brought myrrh for Jesus' burial (John 19:39–40).

Take some time to think about this part of the story of a baby who grew to manhood in hard circumstances and was then 'despised and rejected'. Consider, if you can, for a short while, your own mortality. It seems good to me that we should do this from time to time, though not in a morbid way. What would you regret not having done or said to another if your death were to come sooner than you thought it would? Bring these thoughts to God. Then you may like to use the prayer of abandonment, which we can pray for ourselves at any time, as well as when we think about our mortality.

Father, I abandon myself into
your hands;
   do with me as you will.
Whatever you may do, I accept all.
Let only your will be done in me,
   and in all your creatures—
   I wish no more than this, O Lord.
Into your hands I commend my soul;
   I offer it to you with all the love of
my heart,
   for I love you, Lord, and so need to
give myself,
   to surrender myself into your hands
without reserve,
   and with boundless confidence,
   for you are my father.

CHARLES DE FOUCAULD (1858–1916)

Epiphany is also the time when the lectionary readings deal with the stories of the ways in which Jesus was revealed long after the wise men had gone. They include Jesus the boy in the temple, listening to his elders (Luke 2:41–51), Jesus when he was baptised by John (Matthew 3:13–17) and Jesus and the first miracle at the marriage in Cana (John 2:1–11). You may like to spend some time with these readings, and could perhaps find some symbols to place in your quiet corner. For the visit to the temple, maybe you could use a picture of a child of about Jesus' age, or

something that reminds you of when you were younger, or a time when you travelled somewhere new and previously unknown. For the baptism, a simple bowl of water may suffice, and maybe a ring or a heart for the marriage story.

Light a candle to remind you of the 'light for revelation for the Gentiles and for glory to your people Israel'

So enjoy Epiphany, and, when you reach Candlemas, read Luke 2:22–40. Imagine you are Simeon or Anna holding that baby. Hold the child in your imagination and light a candle to remind you of the 'light for revelation for the Gentiles and for glory to your people Israel' (Luke 2:32).

Sit and look. Sit and wonder. Sit and be.

My Reflections

This space is for you to make your own notes.

On the beach, waiting for the tide to turn

© Heather Fenton 2008

'Give me my scallop shell of quiet'

Sir Walter Raleigh wrote this pilgrimage prayer. Born in England about 1552, he died on 29 October 1618. He is, of course, known for being an explorer but was also a courtier and a poet.

Give me my scallop-shell of quiet,
*   My staff of faith to walk upon,*
My scrip of joy, immortal diet,
*   My bottle of salvation,*
My gown of glory, hope's true gage;
And thus I'll take my pilgrimage.

Blood must be my body's balmer;
*   No other balm will there be given:*
Whilst my soul, like quiet palmer,
*   Travelleth towards the land*
of heaven;
Over the silver mountains,
Where spring the nectar fountains;
*   There will I kiss*
*   The bowl of bliss;*
And drink mine everlasting fill
Upon every milken hill.
My soul will be a-dry before;
But, after, it will thirst no more.

SIR WALTER RALEIGH

Prayer as God's gift

> Prayer has its source and **origin in God...**

This text from *Praying with Paul* by Tom Smail (BRF, 2007) looks at what Paul says about prayer in Romans 8.

author

Tom Smail is a retired college lecturer and church leader who continues to write and preach in the UK and beyond.

It will take the rest of this chapter and all of the next to spell out what [Romans 8:26] means, but the basic point is that authentically Christian prayer starts not with us but with God. It does not originate in our thoughts and desires and then move out from us to make contact with God. On the contrary, the mention of the intercession of the Spirit here underlines the fact that prayer has its source and origin in God: before we offer it to him, he gives it to us. It is the Spirit of God who is the source of our intercession. He comes to us from God, bringing with him into our deep hearts the prayer that we can then make our own and offer back to the God who has given it to us.

What we are saying here has to be seen in the context of the main message of the letter to the Romans. In the earlier chapters, Paul has been making his basic point, over and over again and in many different ways, that, because we are sinners, we cannot attain a right relationship with God by our own efforts to keep his law and obey his commandments. All such efforts at self-justification are doomed to failure. We cannot get into a right relationship with God by relying at all on what we do for him, but rather by relying on what he has done for us in Christ incarnate, crucified and risen. A right relationship with God therefore is a matter not of performance but of reception; it comes to us not as a reward for our own efforts, but as an undeserved gift won for us by God's Son and given for us to receive and enjoy by God's Spirit.

What is said about prayer in Romans 8 is entirely in line with the approach of the whole letter. Because prayer is at the very centre of a right relationship with God, we are here invited to think of prayer not first and foremost as a hard and demanding work to be accomplished but, rather, as a free and gracious gift to be received. Whatever level of theological sophistication we may have reached on the conscious level of our thinking, deep down under the surface in

most of us is the idea that prayer and indeed all worship is something that we must do in order to get in touch with God. According to this view, God is far above us up there in heaven in the transcendence of the Creator over his creatures and in the holiness that separates him from sinners; it is our intimidating task to reach him with our worship and win from him a favourable answer to our prayers. He is, as it were, the target nearly beyond our reach and our prayers are the arrows we fit into the

Because we are sinners, we cannot attain a right relationship with God by our own efforts to keep his law and obey his commandments...

bow of our faith in the uncertain hope of hitting a bullseye. If the metaphor is crude, so also is the theology that it expresses!

Prayer as technique

In such circumstances it is of prime importance to have a bow of faith strong enough to span the distance and an aim accurate enough to make a hit. For this

way of thinking, everything depends on us and our learning the right techniques to win us success. All those questions about whether we have been asking for the right thing for long enough and with sufficient faith loom large—so large that they turn us in on ourselves and our perplexities and thus distract our attention from God, undermining our confidence in his willingness to hear us and his grace to respond to us.

What if prayer were not this kind of hard task that often daunts us, but a free gift graciously given...?

All those questions...

Some fruitful questions

What if prayer were not this kind of hard task that often daunts us, but a free gift graciously given and to be gratefully received? What if it were not the testing means by which we try to reach God but the kind provision that he makes to reach us? What if the answer to the problems we have been thinking about were not for us to solve by schooling ourselves to pray better, but to turn our attention away from ourselves and our efforts and instead to tune in to the perfect prayer that the Spirit is already praying in our hearts? What if the central clue to the whole life of worship and indeed to all Christian living were what Paul says in Galatians 2:20: 'It is no longer I who live, but it is Christ who lives in me'?

When we are getting ready to pray, we should realise that right from the start **we are not on our own**

© INSADCO Photography/Alamy

It can be helpful to make this general statement specific in situations that, if we faced them alone, could worry and disturb us, for example: 'It is no longer I who am going into this difficult interview, but Christ who is going in with me.' In the present context this means that when we are getting ready to pray, we should realise that right from the start we are not on our own: 'It is no longer I who am responsible for what is going to happen in this prayer time, but Christ who will be praying in

me.' It works: again and again I have approached my own morning prayer time with heaviness and reluctance, and again and again I have discovered the mysterious nature of what is going on there—what I have got out of it has been immeasurably more than what I have put into it; my eyes have been opened, my mood has been changed, my hopes have been raised because of his giving to me in my praying to him. Because Paul approaches prayer in that way, he passes over questions of technique almost in silence. For him the issues about how we are to pray are secondary and can be helpfully addressed only when we have tuned in to the nature and character of the God to whom we pray.

The way you conduct any relationship depends on what sort of person you are relating to and it is no different with God. The kind of relationship we can have with a God who is remote and repelling in his holiness will be quite different from the

> The way you conduct any relationship depends on what sort of person you are relating to and it is **no different with God**

relationship we can have with a God who is open and outgoing towards us in his redeeming and transforming love. To find out what Paul has to say to us about how we can pray rightly, we have to look at all he says about the God to whom we pray in the whole of Romans 8.

Prayer and the Trinity

As we do so, we shall see that the relationship with God that, for Paul, makes Christian prayer possible—a relationship expressed by Christian prayer—is much more complex than we might at first have expected. It is in fact a trinitarian relationship. As Gordon Fee puts it, 'In these chapters Paul's trinitarian presuppositions stand out everywhere. God is the prime mover, the principal actor in all things. God has brought about this salvation, this new people for his name, through the death and resurrection of his own Son (8:3). And God has brought all of it to realisation through the gift of his Holy Spirit, who is also the Spirit of his Son' (*God's Empowering Presence*, Paternoster, 1995, p. 517).

Paul did not, of course, have anything like a worked-out doctrine of the Trinity; that came much later. The very nature of the gospel he was exploring, however, led him to the conviction that the God it revealed to us was simultaneously and equally the Father above us, the Son incarnate as one of us and the Holy Spirit working among us and within us. We have only to draw attention to three central verses in Romans 8 to realise that Paul knew perfectly well that the Christian relationship to God was in fact a threefold relationship to a triune God.

In verses 15–17 he speaks of how God the Father is involved in our praying: 'For you did not receive a spirit of slavery to fall back into fear, but you have received a spirit of adoption. When we cry "Abba, Father!" it is that very Spirit bearing witness with our spirit that we are children of God, and if children, then heirs, heirs of God and joint heirs with Christ—if, in fact, we suffer with him so that we may also be glorified with him.' Our relationship to Abba is at the centre of all our praying, but it is at the same time a trinitarian relationship because our access to the Father is made possible only through the Son and in the Spirit.

The role of the incarnate, crucified and ascended Son in our praying is, however, the explicit subject of verse 34 of the same chapter, where Paul speaks of 'Christ Jesus who died, yes, who was raised, who is at the right hand of God, who indeed intercedes for us.' The incarnate Christ is now at the right hand of God and his work there is a perpetual prayer of intercession on behalf of his people. The implication is that, if this is central to his ministry, it will be central to the ministry of all who belong to him as well.

The incarnate Christ is now at the right hand of God and his work there is a perpetual prayer of intercession

God is the prime mover

Alongside there is also a mysterious involvement of God the Holy Spirit in our praying. So verses 26–27, which, as we have seen, speak of our *astheneia* in prayer, also tell of the Holy Spirit's activity deep within our praying to heal our sickness and to remedy our incapacity: 'that very Spirit intercedes with sighs too deep for words. And God who searches the heart knows what is the mind of the Spirit, because the Spirit intercedes for the saints according to the will of God.' The answer to the problems of our praying is the other kind of praying that is simultaneously going on in our hearts and in our midst—the perfect prayer of the Spirit.

Summarising all this in preparation for our detailed expounding of it in the next chapter, we can already devise something like a trinitarian definition of Christian prayer: the Father is the one to whom we pray, the Son is the one with whom we pray and the Spirit is the one in whom we pray. Because these three are one God and so fulfil their different roles in total union and interdependence, in our praying we have ourselves to take account of the distinctive part that each divine person plays within it and indeed within the whole gospel story, which is the context of all Christian praying.

Prayer to the Father

In our praying, as in the whole revealed gospel, the Father is both the source from which everything else comes and the destination to which everything else returns. It is the Father's love for us that starts it all: 'God so loved the world that he gave his only Son' (John 3:16). In his will for restored relationship with us he sends his Son and his Spirit out from his own life into our life and our world so that they, each in his own distinctive way, may bring us back to him.

Jesus says, 'I am the way, and the truth, and the life. No one comes to the Father except through me' (John 14:6). The Son is uniquely and irreplaceably the way to the Father, but the Father, not the Son, is the destination to which we are called to return.

This is also the rule of our praying: 'Through him [Christ] both of us have access in one Spirit to the Father' (Ephesians 2:18). That is exactly what prayer is—access to the Father—and it is at the heart of the distinctive prayer that Jesus gives to his disciples: 'Pray then in this way: "Our Father…"' (Matthew 6:9). That is what Paul is echoing here: 'And by him [the Spirit] we cry "Abba, Father"' (Romans 8:5, NIV).

> He sends his Son and his Spirit
> out from his own
> life into our life

Prayer with the Son

In our praying, just as in the whole revealed gospel, the Son in his incarnation, without ceasing to be God and sharing equally the deity of the Father, is made man and so stands in complete solidarity with us on the human side of our relationship with the Father, dealing with the Father on our behalf. What Paul says here about the intercession of Christ is consonant with that. He is not the one to whom we pray, but his prayer on our behalf and our identification with it give our intercession its confidence and its validity.

Prayer in the Spirit

Again, in our praying just as in the whole revealed gospel, the Holy Spirit is identified as the one who takes what the Father has done on our behalf through the Son and involves us personally and corporately in it. As Jesus promises in John 16:14: 'He [the Spirit] will take what is mine and declare it to you.'

That is in line with how Paul expounds the work of the Spirit in Romans 8. The cry *Abba*, which is first of all the cry of Jesus, becomes in the Spirit our cry: 'God has sent the Spirit of his Son into our hearts, crying "Abba! Father!"' (Galatians 4:6)—a trinitarian statement if ever there was one. It is the same with our intercession: what the Son prays for us at the right hand of the Father (Romans 8:34), the Spirit prays in us at the roots of our being and the bottom of our hearts (v. 29).

To summarise, we have seen that Paul's teaching on prayer in this chapter is intimately related to both the doctrine

> The Father, not the Son, is the destination to which we are called to return...

of salvation by grace that dominates this letter and the whole trinitarian structure of the gospel. The problems of prayer are best addressed when we receive it as the gift of the triune God. That is the basic structure of our praying. In the next chapter we shall begin to see how much help that trinitarian structure offers in the daily reality of our praying.

Christ is risen, alleluia!

Jesus was risen

This is an extract from *Oh God, Why?* by Gerard Hughes (BRF, 2003). For further information, see www.brfonline.org.uk.

author

Gerard Hughes is a Jesuit priest who works ecumenically on spirituality with a particular interest in people actively engaged in justice and peace initiatives.

So Peter set out with the other disciple to go to the tomb. They ran together, but the other disciple, running faster than Peter, reached the tomb first; he bent down and saw the linen cloths lying on the ground, but did not go in. Simon Peter who was following now came up, went right into the tomb, saw the linen cloths on the ground, and also the cloth that had been over his head; this was not with the linen cloths but rolled up in a place by itself. Then the other disciple who had reached the tomb first also went in; he saw and he believed. Till this moment they had failed to understand the teaching of scripture, that he must rise from the dead.

JOHN 20:3–9

[After a Lenten journey of seven weeks, we finally reach the day of resurrection.] Yet in one sense, nothing has changed. If we focus on this scene, it can come as an anti-climax.

I still have the same temperament as on the day I started this journey. I still bear the same wounds, inflicted by others and by myself, probably live in the same place with the same people, have the same job, or lack of it, the same problems to face.

Faith does not change the external world, but it changes the way we perceive it, and it is from change in our perception that external change happens.

In today's Gospel, Peter and John run to the tomb. John gets there first, but hesitates on the outside. Peter rushes straight in. John then follows. 'He saw and he believed.' John saw an empty tomb, a scene of desolation: he believed Jesus was risen.

'Belief', in English, connotes gullibility, acceptance without proof. 'Belief' in the New Testament means much more than the English word can convey. Belief is knowing, but a knowing which is not based solely on observation, inner reasoning, logical deduction, or the assurance of other people. Belief is an inner sensing, more

like an intuition. We cannot create it, manufacture it, or force ourselves into it; all that we can do is be still and discover the gift within ourselves. 'The Spirit of him who raised Jesus from the dead is living in you' (Romans 8:11). This is the reality in which we live. By praying the Gospel scenes imaginatively, we can meet the risen Christ now, living within us and amongst us, pledge of our resurrection.

But how reliable are the Gospel accounts? Was there really an empty tomb? Did Jesus really rise again from the dead? What kind of body did he have? Is there really life after death? If so, what kind of bodies will we have?

These are all very interesting and important questions, but if we start with these questions and try to find satisfactory answers before praying the resurrection scenes, we shall never get started. Accept the resurrection narratives as they are presented in the Gospels, leaving these other questions aside for the moment. This is not intellectual dishonesty, but intellectual humility, an acknowledgment that the resurrection is a mystery into which God alone can lead us, a mystery in which we are now living. Stand with John in the empty tomb, and pray to believe as he believed. Be with the other disciples in the upper room, listen to their fears and tell them of your own. See the risen Christ among you and hear him say to you, 'Peace', as he shows you his wounded hands and side. Imagination can put us in touch with the reality that Christ is risen, that he is our peace. Be with Mary in the garden, recognising him in the gardener. Be with the two disciples on the road to Emmaus and meet him in the stranger. Be still, and hear his Spirit in your heart calling you by name and saying, 'I am closer to you than you are to yourself. I shall never leave you, for you and I are one undivided person.'

Then bring your attention back into the present and look around… The Lord is truly risen, is within us and amongst us. Alleluia!

> Imagination can put us in touch with the reality that Christ is risen, that he is our peace

God be in my head

God be in my head
and in my understanding;
God be in my eyes
and in my looking;
God be in my mouth
and in my speaking;
God be in my heart
and in my thinking;
God be at my end
and at my departing.

You may have sung this little prayer many times. The tune is simple and may be a good 'humming tune', so you could do that while going about your tasks in the house or the garden. It is taken from a Book of Hours, a 1514 service book used in Clare College, Cambridge.

Quiet Spaces subscriptions

Quiet Spaces is published three times a year, in May, September and January. To take out a subscription, please complete this form, indicating the month in which you would like your subscription to begin.

❏ I would like to take out a subscription myself

Name _____

Address_____

Postcode_____ Telephone Number _____

Email _____

❏ Please do not send me further information about BRF publications.

❏ I would like to give a gift subscription (please complete your name and address above and details of the person you want to give a subscription to below)

Gift subscription name _____
Gift subscription address _____

_____

_____ Postcode _____

Please send beginning with the Jan 11 / May 11 / Sep 11 issue: (delete as applicable)

(please tick box)   UK   SURFACE   AIR MAIL

Quiet Spaces   ❏ £16.95   ❏ £18.45   ❏ £20.85

Please complete the payment details below and send this coupon, with payment to: BRF, 15 The Chambers, Vineyard, Abingdon OX14 3FE.

Method: ❏ Cheque (payable to BRF) ❏ Mastercard ❏ Visa ❏ Maestro

Card no. ☐☐☐☐ ☐☐☐☐ ☐☐☐☐ ☐☐☐☐ ☐☐☐☐

Valid from ☐☐☐☐ Expires ☐☐☐☐ Issue no. of Maestro card ☐☐☐

Security Code ☐☐☐

Signature _____ Date ____ / ____ / ____

All orders must be accompanied by the appropriate payment.

BRF is a Registered Charity   PROMO REF: QSTOMORROW

To order *Quiet Spaces* or other BRF publications mentioned in this journal, visit your local Christian bookshop or go to BRF's website www.brfonline.org.uk.

Resourcing your spiritual journey with brf

Something new happens with the next two issues of *Quiet Spaces* on 'Bread for the journey' and 'A light for my path'. The first one for 2012, entitled 'Sit' will be the first of three Olympic themes.

Next issue

Look out for the next issue, *Bread for the journey*, available from March 2011.
978 184101 830 0

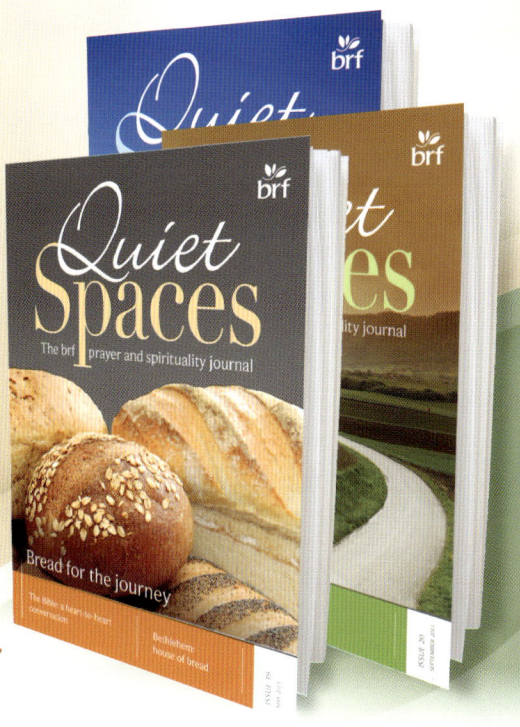

Quiet Spaces, the prayer and spirituality journal from BRF, is an ideal resource for all those who wish to enrich their spiritual and prayer life.

You will want to dip in to *Quiet Spaces* time and time again to appreciate the articles, poetry and images— a wealth of material for thought and reflection.

A wonderful source for meditation and prayer…

SISTER FRANCES DOMINICA, FOUNDER AND TRUSTEE HELEN & DOUGLAS HOUSE

2011/12 issues

Bread for the journey	978 184101 830 0	£4.99
A light for my path	978 184101 831 7	£4.99
Sit	978 184101 832 4	£4.99

Other issues available

Yesterday	978 184101 659 7	£4.99
Today	978 184101 660 3	£4.99
Tomorrow	978 184101 661 0	£4.99
Morning	978 184101 540 8	£4.99
Noon	978 184101 541 5	£4.99
Night	978 184101 542 2	£4.99
Solitude	978 184101 598 9	£4.99
Community	978 184101 599 6	£4.99
Nation	978 184101 600 9	£4.99
The City	978 184101 483 8	£4.99

Available from your local Christian bookshop or, in case of difficulty, from BRF **www.brfonline.org.uk** 01865 319700

Quiet Spaces

In this issue

Tomorrow remains in some senses a mystery but we can prepare for it. 'Seeking one's place of resurrection' is Andrew's contribution, while Jim offers us a meditation on letting go. Marion knows that living in today but being aware of tomorrow is not always easy, and David helps us to look at what is perhaps the greatest image of new creation.

A wonderful source for meditation and prayer...

Let those who risk taking 'time out' to read *Quiet Spaces* be filled with the wonder, awe and beauty of what God presents to them each day.

www.quietspaces.org.uk

brf

978-1-84101-661-0

UK £4.99

9 781841 016610

visit the **brf** website at www.brf.org.uk

Photograph: Image Source Black/Alamy   Design: Louise Blackmore

Quiet Spaces

The brf prayer and spirituality journal

Tomorrow

ISSUE 18 JANUARY 2011

Journeying together to seek our place of resurrection

More than just another day

Prayer and Spirituality Resources

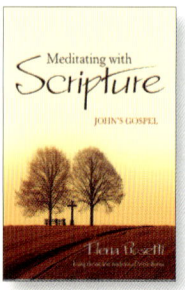

Meditating with Scripture: John's Gospel

Elena Bosetti

A verse-by-verse commentary on John's Gospel, *Meditating with Scripture* is a useful introduction to the discipline of *lectio divina* ('sacred reading'). Each of the twelve chapters concludes with exercises and a meditation.

pb, 978 1 84101 823 2, £7.99

Growing a Caring Church

Wendy Billington

An entry-level guide to pastoral care for churches who want to be church for one another. Explaining in simple terms some of the essential and practical pastoral skills which boost the emotional well-being of a congregation, the book shows how home groups can be the basis for pastoral care.

pb, 978 1 84101 799 0, £6.99

Seasons of the Spirit

Teresa Morgan

Reflections on experiencing the cycle of the Church's year, from one Advent to the next, interwoven with poetic meditations and gentle spiritual lessons drawn from parish life in a historic village church on the edge of Oxford.

pb, 978 1 84101 710 5, £6.99

The Promise of Easter

Fleur Dorrell

Accessible undated, Bible-based reading for the weeks of Lent looking at six themes: holiness, relationship, forgiveness, sacrifice, hope and love. Each reading comprises a Bible passage, comment, spiritual exercise, prayer and final point for reflection to encourage application of the message to daily life.

pb, 978 1 84101 788 4, £4.99